MOZART'S STARLING

MOZART'S STARLING

Ralph Burns

```
PS
3552
.U732493
M69
1990
```

Copyright © 1990
All rights reserved

Publication of this book has been aided by a grant
from the Ohio Arts Council.
Manufactured in the U.S.A.

Design: Joyce Barlow Dodd
Composition: BookMasters, Ashland, Ohio

Some of these poems have appeared in these magazines, to which grateful
acknowledgment is made:
The Atlantic (Barbed Wire)
Field (Texas Aubade, Mozart's Starling, For Luck under the title Luck, Influence)
The Ohio Review (Luck, The Distance)
Ploughshares (The Shimmer of Influence)
Poetry, copyright 1987 and 1988 (The Comfort of a Woman, Lullaby, Debris)
Yankee (Stars)

The author wishes to express
Special thanks to the Arkansas Art Council.

Library of Congress Cataloging in Publication Data

Burns, Ralph, 1949–
   Mozart's starling : poems / Ralph Burns.
    p.   cm.
   "An Ohio Review Book."
   ISBN 0-942148-13-4 : $15.95.——ISBN 0-942148-12-6 (pbk.) : $8.95
   I. Title.
PS3552.U732493M69 1990
811'.54——dc20   90-7239
                                                                   CIP

for Candace and William

CONTENTS

I
INFLUENCE

Influence	5
The Shimmer of Influence	9
The Persistence of Influence	11
The Anxiety of Influence	13

II
WILL

Barbed Wire	17
Texas Aubade	18
Mozart's Starling	19
The Least Circumference	21
Will	23

III
THE STRINGS

The Comfort of a Woman	27
Stars	28
Paul's Sentence	30
The Strings	31
Lullaby	33

IV
LUCK

The Surprise Lilies of Plural, Arkansas	37
Debris	38
For Luck	40
Luck	43

V
LETTER TO MY SON

Easter Water	53
The Distance	54
Creeping Determinism	59
The Man in the Boy's Storm	60

NOTES   63

MOZART'S STARLING

I
INFLUENCE

Influence

I remember Ken Bottoms leaning
on the iron railing of the steps
to some kind of fundamentalist
church. Just after my father's funeral.

They had worked in the same lab as marine biologists.
Best friends. Then over something
I never quite figured out,
grave enemies.

It seemed they argued over who was smarter
or who had the most valid education
or maybe who was stronger
or who messed around most

on his wife. "Ralph?" he said,
smilingly, and he stuck out his hand,
a strong grip I remembered.
Then I remembered Ken used to wrestle.

"Ralph, you haven't changed much."
Well, I could hardly see.
I could hardly stand up.
When I opened my mouth to speak

a huge bubble hobbled forth.
Then, as if it suddenly hit him,
Ken said, "Just two days ago
my son and his wife had their

first child." And he was plainly happy.
His first grandchild was making
his entry just as my father
was leaving, his grandchild

by the gentle hands of the small
town obstetrician, my father
by his own fierce hand.
Thereafter, Ken tipped his hat,

it was green felt.
He walked away—
over the St. Augustine,
across the steaming blacktop.

He patted his right front pocket, jangled
out his car keys, opened the steel door,
slid into his seat, started up
and drove, drove off straight,

straight as the sun's green teeth.
And that was the last time I saw Ken.
I don't know what to think
about it—his news was wonderful news,

the light in his eyes was real,
not meant to further perplex.
But he didn't acknowledge
the immediate situation, either,

nor that my father was a presence
in his life—That was all I saw
of him. His turning to leave
too happily. His driving away.

Influence is like oxygen,
it's in the room with you.
So I found myself walking
into Peck's Bar

with my son in my arms
and the crowd there invasively
friendly—a bar
my father might've liked,

round bulbs over the moose,
shuffleboard powdered with corn meal,
the slam of dominoes, loud conversation
building from experience. "Life ain't fair."

"No, not at all." "Brenda just
started nursing school." "That don't
make her worth a shit." "My experience
with the Leboyer Method was

the greatest experience of my life."
"Why is it, when you date them
they want to go out drinking
every night, but when you marry

them it's a crime."
An elderly, distinguished-looking man
offered to buy me a beer, and to hold
my son for a while. To remember.

He leaned and touched my arm—
"My daughter died six weeks ago," he said.
"She was thirty-five. . . . It's okay,"
he assured me, "it's been six weeks."

Simply that, and he went on
with his imitation of my son's
sounds, but his notes were
pitched higher and more and more

lost. So what is that bad music,
what is the frequency response
residing in the dead leaves
caught in the sugar maple,

when they rattle with the wind but
can't make a sound. Or make
only one sound. That particular,
ordinary, scraping sound

which doesn't care if we listen.

The Shimmer of Influence

Last night my wife brought my son into bed,
to sleep between us fitfully, his hunger
having startled him awake. He kneaded
the air then held on fast to my finger.

All day I'd walk from some new anger
or other, trace my own steps, imagine wrongs.
I'd walk room to room forgetting things—
table to office back to table.

From somewhere in the future my son waves goodbye.
Goodbye to me, empty
as all people are empty,
but waving him goodbye,

wishing he'd drive carefully for Christ's sake.
The open road slides under him.
His hands open and close on the wheel.
Goodbye to his mother, who fed and kept him warm

and laid him down between us some nights
which she told him of, cooingly,
so that now he's embarrassed.
I see him waving all at once all the time

but I don't see the pure terror of it,
not the heave, the real letting go
Ben Jonson spoke of, claiming
he could lose all father now.

I remember leaning out of the window
of the Ford Fairlane as I backed away slowly
from the white house, over the gravel,
cursed my own father and laughed

as he beat the air and cursed me back, calling
me nothing, the dead air alive with invention.
I enter his brain like a bullet
and look now for an exit.

I remember the sound of gravel, the punctuation,
the dull rumination of it under my tires.
Goodbye. Goodbye to the shimmer of Highway Six.
Goodbye to the father waving and whistling,

out on the drive now, out in the street.
Goodbye to the son as I walk him out the door,
outside, around a house defined
by two trees, a hedge, and a driveway

leading off into the weeds. Soon
he's asleep on my shoulder, my son
William whom I named my father's name.
I feel the spooky silk of his palm.

The Persistence of Influence

As I pack our son for the ride across town
to the babysitter, up the hill of aisled kudzu,
due west, I think of Telemachus rounding up
the Ithacans, setting out in the opposite
direction to find his lost father, Odysseus;
and beg out this time, clipping and watering
the hedge instead. How long can this last,
my walking past the same behavior of light?
Particles bend according to their size,
white light breaking to color. I hear you,
Billie, still singing, canning beets
and pickling eggs. I feel a final splash
of sun after having dragged the Louisville Slugger
through the red clay alleys of Tulsa, Oklahoma,
the power in the wide open vowels of my family,
for a time. I sit on the inner ash wood sill,
one son of many, most tactical father,
call out over the sweet green stems,
past the line of fence,
the flowering tree,
the sour daylight damp,
to the doorway,
to the middle of the ladder,
to the yellow green grasses
that stretch forever.

I remember but probably invent
the pink streaming clouds
of dawn, the armor inside,
the cuirass and ankle chains,
a solid job, a budget I can count on.

I wanted to see you one more time, Uncle,
ghosting across the wood floor of Dowd Seed and Grain,
then settling at one end of the counter,
fist on hip, elbow cocked,
talking baseball as if
you spoke of a past infinitely divisible.

I only wanted to pick up the five iron
and walk out to where the yellow brush
waved and waved and parted itself freely
like breakers in the salt immortal sea.

The Anxiety of Influence

I've been dying to repeat that corny maxim:
don't judge another Indian till you've walked
a mile in his moccasins; but couldn't work it
in the conversation. Maybe because

I can't hear it again boldly or
retrieve it from the fiber optics,
that reference to someone essentially you
and me. I know the folly of wishing for ignorance—

you get it. And likewise, silence.
Yesterday a man whom I suspect,
who I think suspects me, gave me
a list of regrets—knots

in a rope he climbs daily, starting
in the lumbar region, baffling
forth until the last thing
he says floats beyond him: don't judge me.

I'd telephone if I could,
I'd punch out the right harmonics
just to hear you, even the hallucination
that we can live forever in ignorance like animals,

all those maxims and gruff directives meant
to guide the wanderer, or simply
to mention the possibility of swerve
as atoms collide with atoms, or simply

to pass along love of father to son
who for too long stares at one place,
his own splay stance on
the airport linoleum and the dancing, internal

shapes within each square, waltzing
their miles. I'm sick of the poetry
of self, like those old croons
in the ears of the stalwart crowd listening

to Jack Shelton. How terrible to pretend
submission to music. How terrible
to remember forward especially,
to have nothing to be able to undo,

to sit with nothing in the mouth.
I remember something funny you said,
how you were most colorful
in a line of crazies. And you *were* lovely—

I know that now—who submitted fully
to time, who knew of some scene
when you were alive with others
as though by design. A stranger walked in.

But you were genius of the place.
You played moon at a far table.
Traffic floated by on Texas Avenue.
In the middle of something seemingly unrelated

you turned to Angie,
who pulled a drafted from behind the bar,
Honey, you said,
you make my love muscle grow.

II
WILL

Barbed Wire

Two or more strands twisted together,
oxides and baser salts, admixture
of carbon, metal of lash and scourge,
strung like a virus, barbed intervals,

stapled by hand to bois d'arc poles,
woven by machine, "devil's rope"
of vast interior plains,
of meadows bruised by their own

amplitude, barbed wire of a thousand
different kinds, undulating loops,
half round and square—Reynold's Web,
Preston's Braid, Meriwether's Cold-

Weather Wire, Shellaberger's Long Zigzag,
Walking Wire, Curtis' Ladder, Visible Lace,
Arch and Leaf, Descending Beads, Staple Barb,
Open Diamond Point, Sproul's Twins,

Elsey's Ribbon, Brink's Buckle, Ellwood's Star,
Flute and Rib, Spool and Spurs, Joined Saucers,
Tie through Eye, Body Grip,
Blake's Knee Grip, Underwood's Tack—

unloved, unloving; that to name these
does no political good, but as precision
is polemical, against vague statement
and circular evasion, as the sharp angle of sun

and crossed wires together body forth a spark,
it is some kind—cold, unmusical, utterly itself—
keeping cattle in, or the enemies of sheep
out.

Texas Aubade

The bluebonnets, paintbrushes, evening primrose,
the solid roll of the Zephyr, two whistles, trailing
smoke above the far wood, the nickel
on the track wide as a dollar, the straining plenum
of the udder witholding its drip, the calf who called
all night in the pasture, who was called
by its mother, both feigning confusion in an eternal
game of keep away, the blue spruce mist of late March,
sun coming on like that brush fire of Lucian's

which spanned a football field; and the witness,
and the assist of—Lee who seemed permanent,
bark on the tree, who sat for years on the same
barstool, third from the left; Jim, wounded
in the war, whose arm still bled; Lois with her
battery-operated fan; Benito who worked for
the railroad. All prove what nobody denies.
And the cattle munching coastal bermuda are so.
They scratch mightily against the fence.

And Carl who sang in a band, who when any
band played—country, bohemian, Czech—wanted
to sing Bill Bailey. His voice and their voices
double in the tumble of hill and wildflower,
dramatic reds and oranges and blues; and green,
for simplicity. How steadily it moves,
the shadow over the grass.
How intricate the play of light and shadow.
How each leaf is less, each pull of the grass.

Mozart's Starling

We can't be sure. Did Mozart
learn the theme from his starling?
Or the other way around?

I side with the maestro.
That damn 17th is too complex
for a single bird, and it's too

much for the Czech band which is
tuning up inside a dome in Milano,
Texas where the ceiling has been

lowered and the walls covered
with paneling. The old dentist
"Doc" Kruse shows up with his young

72-year-old girl and they polka
under the rickety ceiling fans
which also hold light, permitting

a pale bluster. Too much, maybe,
for a bird. And what about the crow
which arrives every year for the next

seven and sits on a fence post which
has been recently painted, first
with aluminum primer, then

with a whiter white than I can imagine,
just to rest for a pretty minute?
The music says to take my wine

outside and look up at the stars
which fall just now, two at once,
in private arrangement.

It says try and tell the truth,
if it's interesting.

The Least Circumference

I will stop talking about my father.
Like the wasp who dove into the earth,
descend lower. For the reason
that it's raining and a lovely

asphalt smell. Yesterday you wrote
with the antique fountain pen
we bought you for your birthday
describing your own father who retired

in the 60's, brought his files home,
and changed the bedroom to an office,
where you stay this month, help
if need be, in time of sickness,

in time of despair; and you found
this beautiful paper, "tired old yellow"
you call it. The life and death of
this house seemed safe and beyond;

but you're faithful to its living thought,
and to history, which stopped there
some forty-odd years ago,
as you left home after high school,

letting the screen door slam.
You were capable of the fullest circumference
then. But the way changed;
and the chances, as you stepped them off,

as you made and limited them,
changed. You write in script from a hard-
backed chair in your father's room
which used to be a bedroom;

and the fountain pen makes its voyage
with just the right compression.
Your fingers have left some sweat spots,
or something, on the envelope

and on the paper; and I miss you,
a big wind slams with all the wind it can;
and I need your courage
to remember, as you chide me

in your last paragraph through the voice
of Dickinson: "To hope with imagination
is inevitable—but to remember with it
is the most consecrated ecstasy of the will."

for Edith Wylder

Will

That's what we'll call you, William O'Neil.
I know that I'm too comfortable on Linwood,
in a city where the realtors explain
the neighborhoods are safe, meaning white.
I put straw on top of fescue and water it,
to remember a thing that I've forgotten,
the certainty of green in September,
when school would start. Will,
Sweet William, long in wilderness,
named after your grandfather and your
corny, Bible-thumping uncle,
wild and sweet, a purple spotted spindle
which creeps gradually into the low woods
and the riverbed and overtakes the byway.

Will is a word which won't sit still even now,
as a noun, because of a certain curvature
of spine, a gentle, candid curiosity
that weighs in the womb like a question.
Because will is the end of power,
and the beginning of desire, the power
of choice in regard to action.

It proceeds by wish, longing, loving,
by inclination. An ample kick, a sidelong,
sure-footed feeling outward—Thou wilt,
you will jump down, as the Cherokees say,
whenever you are ready.
                Listen,
I have no will to wander out of doors,
I'm sure of things but afraid to say them;
beyond good and evil, I accuse,
I accuse the attitude of mind directed

to some action. And I've known
a boundless will to please, which isn't
love or charity but a cellular division
of power and mystery, small as
a blade of grass that splits apart.

Your mother touches with fingertips
the precious flower of her belly,
then strokes it absently while talking
or stares at the effect of movement inside.
The hot day cools, the squares
and rectangles subdue to sweetness,
the night falls, falling
through the trees with random improvisation
like a ribbon. There's a woman
inside a house on a street lined with trees
where the trash gets picked up on Tuesdays
and Fridays, where sleep and ignorance
combine and drift out of sight according
to the law of inertia. The lights
go out in the house.
The small heart of the neighborhood blinks out.

III
THE STRINGS

The Comfort of a Woman

Last night I woke to the smell of furnace gas.
I dreamt you'd asked Charlotte to marry you
and told me after we'd tied
to a cyprus stump at Lake Conway,
after the bait-man had filled his plastic tubes
with crickets, then shook them down in our basket,
his hands shaking. You simply said, I love her.
You simply said, She's lovely, blonde, petite.
In reality, her hair's auburn, she's big-boned.

We cast out blue nylon. Three mallards
shook the gnats and mosquitoes loose from
mesquite leaves. When we oared away
you told me why the females are drab
—because they nest and need
camouflage. When I returned to bed, my own
wife warm beside me, I tried to dream you good
fortune, whatever is good, a woman blonde
as a sunfish, small-boned as a sparrow.

Stars

I sit and rock my son to sleep. It rains
and rains. Such as we are
both asleep, we swim past the stars,
bad stars of disaster, good stars of the backbone

of night. We know these stars as they are
and as we'd wish them to be, Milky Way,
Dog and Bear, hydrogen and helium, the 92
elements which make all we know of beauty.

We know nothing of angular size or
of the inverse square law of the propagation
of light, and swim through a cold, thin
gas, between and among the stars,

which swim likewise between two creations
like children who know sleep intimately.

*

First the collapse of the interstellar gasses,
then the final collapse of the luminous stars
like eyes turning backward in their sockets
returning the atoms they have synthesized

back into space, to dust, back to what they were.
We look from some kind of opening to nothing.
We locate the red giant and the dwarf star
for nothing. They are going away—

their explosions from within and their luster,
their mixed-up views on time and space.
I know that those I love are some
of the falling objects, and those dark waves

rise toward us from the past, dark
that falls with any particle of light.

Paul's Sentence

There's the one about how you and your
wife decided finally to split, how piece
by piece your daughter helped you carry
your furniture to the van, and quietly,
she rounded one corner of the house
and daylight hung in strips, and stepping
beautifully over small grass, lifted
a revolver to her temple and all
the sweet everything of everything
terrible and all the littleness
and great clatter of the leaves
spoke its language as she spoke hers
from a language which you and her mother
had some say in, listened to and gave
a certain rondure, and now
you speak loudly, laugh out
of time, and we who work with
and pass you in the halls,
walk past a grief beyond which
is no enduring, no closing small
as a fist, talking our talk
like a memory of faces mocking
faces, an honest inversion
of people and things which we
kindly refer to as office politics.

The Strings

Too thin to see, so thread-like they
extend millions of light years back.
They seem sentimental the way
the mind relives itself, how forgetting
is the one true anguish; they seem falsely
continuous—like standing weeds and wide sky,
one father helping with the string,
box kite rising, ringing.

That I may understand, I wake, as I know
you wake across town, many times, unable
to sift the day's recordings.
You open a window. And the four people
in your house breathe in and out of sleep,
who had once been alone. Open a window
and wind cruises through the house
like a child's drawing of flame, light blue,

unrealistically narrow and sharp at the ends
but holding glow, slowing oxidation
pulling one from cold dark
into proximity of people, real and remembered,
sentences speaking regret—remembered,
friendship, betrayal remembered, responsibility, love.
But you stand or sit at the window screen.
I think I see you looking as I look out,

lifting one hand as if to wave.
Just now,
behind a wall of glass (like in front
of the elevators, glass that Sartre
claims keeps us from knowing)

I think I see—from behind this glass
and one live branch—
the profile of head, shoulders, hand

raised in act of erasure. Waving, that is.
So I wave back. And the pane
has in it something of friendship—
that is to say, something from the past
and from the future. That is, an attempt
to see, a way of looking.
That is, a longing to see across the dark.

Lullaby

The upland falls behind the house,
live and scrub oak, barbed wire
firmly implanted stringing unlikely
trees together, terrace by terrace,
down and down, white rock
gleaming through the green.

The art of memory, they say,
is to forget. So sleep now,
smile and sleep and let me
think, sleep past the molecules
of grief, let me kneel and believe,
believe and submit.

Soon enough you'll know hunger,
then sweetness, then a sweet
hunger for what reaches
out to touch. Soon, too,
those poor, nerveless times,
those times when you curse

and strike out at yourself,
when you count up wrongs
and feed them as if they were
one prairie fire. As I sit
and watch you sleep,
I grow angry too

at my abstraction of your sorrow,
at its necessity, at the very idea
of what I cannot speak,
it's so unspeakable.
So sleep and smile,
sleep deep.

IV
LUCK

The Surprise Lilies of Plural, Arkansas

This special alignment of sympathy
and despair, this sticking-out
orange head of it—not only do we not
speak thoughtfully of our time, we
do not speak musically or warningly
like plastics made to swoon like flowers,
do not address God, though we cower
every day, do not doubt out loud or say
I am stuck, I am afraid,
I fear that I do not fear
enough and know enough
and pretend not to know
the little that I do, that I care only for effect
and not the world of things, sudden or exact,
and not the world of spirit, lilium,
trumpet of sky, lilium convallium,
massing the ravine.

Debris

By 10:30 the trash truck has digested our
debris, old hamburger meat, the sour
melon Jim bought, and the cat is scavenging
the linoleum for another meal, which

my wife says is a result of variable interval
reinforcement, producing high
resistance to extinction. (See, we fed him yesterday
at 10:30.) I'm writing on the dining room table

across from my reflection in the mirror
above the buffet. Why can't I look myself
in the eye for more than a few seconds?
I haven't killed anyone. I put

my clothes on like everyone else
and drink a cup of coffee.
I mull over the steam for what awakens,
what survives among the lost connections.

Years ago I listened,
only listened when my father phoned
long distance and said whatever else I love you.
I didn't say a word so

why am I talking now? Why talk so much
now? I started this thing out funnily, didn't I?
A couple of lines about the charm
of domesticity, then I leaned deliberately

on the wall
of the past, the self-inflicted death I've never been
angry at, not obviously, not where I knew anyway
like they say in the self-help manuals.

First you grieve, then you're angry.
But I'm still cloistered in my own black guilt,
still unfocused, a warble in the shrubs.
So why am I talking now?

And why am I talking about talking?
When he called and spoke his love
I only listened and laughed
a shrugging, invulnerable laugh,

who kills himself thoroughly, again and again,
who puts the .410 to his chin and it's
drizzling outside and the phone rings
and we're sleeping.

For Luck

One of us threw an empty soup can out
onto busy Sheridan Avenue for the dog
to chase after. He'd do anything.

It was the first time I'd seen the twitch
and tingle, the trembling that comes just
before death. We pulled him to the side

and he stared at the sky and the sky went
down, like always. All that summer all
I ever wanted was to pitch, run, hit, and catch.

The sounds of cars whirled in the wind
for days. They were real but they grow quiet.

*

I've heard the retina holds an image for
one-sixteenth of a second, that what
we respond to is not light

but light falling, the electromagnetic spectrum
we think of as light. Not knowing, uninformed,
I hauled my Rawlings mitt through traffic,

through rain turning to snow,
and if I had a grown man's thought,
it never occurred to me

to let what was hidden
remain hidden.

*

Wish me luck, we say, and off we go.
Back home, luck is what they wish, and possibility,
an attitude of honesty toward possibility.

When you turn from the river because
the river is cold, or because it reminds
you of home, pick up a rock and hold it

because it is cold, small, rolled in on itself.
Now aren't you better? Don't you feel good?
You have made your own bald luck.

This is your home now.

*

Last week, in my new Kentucky home, I heard
on the tube that two grown men who
were policemen got drunk and drove to
a parking lot to quick-draw. Luckily,
no harm was done, but both had to resign.

And lucky for us they aren't now cruising
the streets keeping the streets intact.
Still, your heart goes out to them.
Will the mind ever heed its mindless asking,
"How's a guy to have any fun?"

*

A field in Tulsa, Oklahoma, in mud. The air
smells of carbon. I dig in the mud for the old
dog's skull. To take it home
to my own backyard where, if luck will
have it, it grows.

And I think the old man was right
when he complained that his choices
kept choosing him. In my yard,
mimosa and poplar, burnt elm,
sycamore, ash, and magnolia.

Luck

Scrub oak and tumbleweed,
I have to go back, sycamore,
ash, and magnolia, the way
you do, in circular bands
of small straight lines, longitude and latitude,
of declination and perpetual apparition,
whose center is everywhere, whose
circumference, nowhere:
The air smells of carbon, let it.
The stringer of fish swims away.
So do the salt and pepper hills
of northern Oklahoma, the red sky
and the red dirt, and the coal pits,
so do the company cars of the fifties,
so does the dog I buried, the skull
I dug back up and buried again.
So do the accidents of heart, the preferences
of passion, the vast need to include all that appears
like hope, like an ecstasy of will and memory,
swim away.

The heron lifts its white weight over the lilies,
then glides over water, and on my scalp
I've felt it, that hand in the world
which is grace. And the heron flaps away.

Over the bald cypresses.
Over the calm, brown water.
And I have to find where to go
like someone being ushered in to a wedding.

Past the Bickell house, beyond Pine Street,
with only myself, a couple

of firecrackers and a cherry bomb,
I scouted what we called the coal pits,

dug by real men
and real machines in the same
syrupy heat I played in.

I climbed the hills of slate and malachite
in clothes camouflaged. Below was
the mosquito-ridden water I could drink
if I had to,
and above, the edible sparrow.

The whole place became a mission,
though the town and suburbs where
servility slept
are also an occasion for reconnaissance.

I edged to the ridge but I think I thought it then:
that possibility is only so much air,
only a flower with a yellow center
surrounded by white petals.

Only a flower, and only one at that.
That, and two basal leaves, and my own echo

bouncing around, while I looked down, enacting
memory itself, not light, but light falling.

That first memory, two or three,
peering through the whitewashed

two-by-four railing on the second-
story pine porch and someone on

the ground whose high-pitched call
probably saved me from falling

or frightened me closer to the edge
so that now on any runway

I must think of something else.
So goes simple cause and effect.

When one thing combines with another
but does not alter or elide, simply

recurs with last year's burdens.
And what about the motion of a created thing

which has nothing to do with time, or
the measure of that motion. What about

that crazed bear who lifts one paw to heaven
and swings his great head in the same

circular plane so that now the motion is frozen
as a law of Pascalian geometry.

What about the unambiguous instant
the lumbar caves in, and the bodily

frame unhinges, and the world
distances itself from the stars

for business purposes.

For it, for the world, we turn cold, then passionate.
Like Yeats' fisherman in Connemara clothes,

who loves and doesn't think, or thinks
and feels in a back-and-forward arc,
flick of the wrist and part of a circle, too,
of father and son, past, present, and future.
A down-turn of the wrist, a fly drops
in the stream, a small and private
pool, widening, including stars and moon,
man and woman, God if you believe,
including earlier creation, the echo
of shod horses a century ago,
the living men that I hate, the dead man
that I hate and love, the men and women
who do not exist, the Oklahoma water,
land, hardwood, and granite, syllabled
to me for names: Chickasaw and Choctaw
from the east, Seminole from Florida,
Cherokee from Georgia and North Carolina,
Quapaw from Arkansas; and the water
was brown, then red, like a hateful cliché,
and the Five Civilized Tribes of Oklahoma:
Cherokee of the Iroquoian, Choctaw and Chickasaw
of the Creek, Seminole of Muskhogean,
Quapaw of the Sioux; and the fish rose up
to meet them, silver apples for the moon,
golden apples for the sun,
a rise pooling out and beyond, ebb
and flow of night sky, encircling
heartwood and thicket, scud and sparkle,
the couple passing under the stars,
white sap rising, sap in the rock,
marrow of air, fire and water,
blood and marrow, flesh and fur.
And one star came streaking down
like a pencil drawing of a single lash.
And the stars swam out to the sea.
One by one, they died, we saw them fall around us,

their skeletal forms borne away by the other stars.
Above the bridge we crossed on Tuesday,
or over the water with the Cherokee name,
they didn't belong to us, but we spoke them—
Oolaga, Spavinaw, Okmulgee,
charging the water and the land.
The names intoxicate, but they're not mine.
Have I danced along the Chisolm?
Have I walked far, very far?
Have I wept through the eyes of the dead?
Have I danced and wept with my dead father?

The problem is the backward motion,
the angle of the cast and reach, the arc
of person and tense, of telling
a story and having none.

Boethius said all things rejoice in their return
to their own nature. Jaymack Norwood said one
more time, walk by this place, I break your fucking
nose. . . .

He slumbers down Sheridan Avenue past the burled
oaks. He walks to the mall and keeps on walking.
Past the new bypass.
Past the mounds of crushed rock.

He picks up a brick and whacks it with a board.
He savors the sound of glass breaking like applause.
And sometimes, where the sidewalks halt: a sewer pipe big enough
for a boy to sleep in, then to wake in

and watch the dissonant gases
engorge one edge of the city.
Dissonance leads to discovery,
though he'd hardly admit it

even to himself, though there may issue
a contaminant, an acculturation, from whence
luck dances its fancy dance, shimmers
awhile before bursting, shimmers and glistens

like the Indians of Anadarko marking
their spot on the earth;
and even though he'd hardly admit it
Santayana claimed that the city is second body

for the mind but more rational, permanent,
and decorative, a work of natural
and moral art where the soul sets up
her trophies of action and instruments of pleasure.

Toward the last, my father referred to his sons
as his boys, and now, today, as I cast blame,
his light heart haunts me.
I've been cruelly aloof,
suspicious, afraid of love, of those who love me most.

Such thoughts recur at the strangest times.
During friendly conversation, before and during
sex, before sleep—
that soft clouds may have murderous intent,
that I may too because I am human.

How that vowel opens though, his *boy*,
then breaks down, gliding off to another,
leaving its distinct character,
without condition.

Leaving the gray wind of Oklahoma,
the hollow soup cans which dance
like the Okies did once
around the bonfire on their way to California.

Dance in the street or on any dirt road.
A downhill dance, and all the way home.
The cats and dogs going crazy.
The traffic getting louder and more real.

And every particle of mass of a man
attracts each particle of mass
on earth, or drifts away.
From voltage aware of itself

as chaos, as a new kind of pity
which turns its back on society,
from the tradition of Homer—
that of having heroes, voyages,

of telling stories and having no story.
There is no mystery
in luck, it's the tale of the tribe.
It begins in a shopping mall in Tulsa,

crosses the busy street of human error
and ends at the light.
The wave falls and the hand falls,
and the force weakens inversely

as the square of the distance between them
and all the bodies of the earth
fall with the same constant acceleration.
Inside, it's indolence, outside

the heavenly bodies bemused.
At our idea of relationship.
Because we seem to care, and caring,
brighten and disappear.

V
LETTER TO MY SON

> My love is my weight.
> —*Augustine*

> I believe in the value of suffering, so long as one makes every (legitimate) effort to escape it.
> —*Simone Weil*
> *Pre-War Notebook*
> *(1933–(?) 1939)*

Easter Water

My two year old son runs the faucet
just to watch—he doesn't disrupt water
by putting his hands in it—egg-caked
hands, water at full-tilt. Years
from now, unable to remember, hearing a knocking
from somewhere as though against a wood
support beneath a fishing dock, the water
cool, dark and deep, the surface rich
and smoky, he'll gaze as he gazes now
unable to act but hearing himself think:
Non fui, fui, non sum, non curo:
I was not, I was, I am not, I do not care.
For now he lets the water fall, all
that now is fallen rise to life again.

The Distance

> La distance immense que separe le
> necessaire et le bien.
> —*Simone Weil*

William has emptied his toy box; he stands amid his work
slightly crooked, pooping.
He doesn't want to use the potty like Millie
Marsh, his literary heroine,
but does demand privacy like that gorgeous whooping
crane which flew nonstop over Europe's
farms and then the Baltic Sea.
As in most migrations
not all of his friends survived
or made it back. I hear his high whispering call.
He bends in the knees or on one knee standing,
the elements which make him,
my elements,
debris cast up like all the loss of Normandy.

*

Small figure beyond my reach, it's funny:
meaning nothing you mean everything:
I imagine you older,
old
as our neighbor John who forgets and leaves
his cane propped against our steps where
he stood moments ago
surveying his repair of the porch ceiling
where wood had rotted
and rain had drizzled coffee- and rust-colored.
So why will John Hemphill be taken
by cancer in bone and blood,
and why
does wind blow your hair in the future,
glancing off this wall?

You make a strange figure, whom
I love absolutely, in ignorance and fear.
Feel my hand in your hair wishing
for return,
for the ability to fly
out of the dark to inhabit this moment.
And so, and so it goes—.
That beauty lives elsewhere.
That distance
between us is immense.

*

My friend's father survives the one in a million odds.
I get off on the Bonne Terre exit
and enter Missouri;
I enter my friend's quirky ability of finding
some sweet angle of panic,
and I wonder if I've got what it takes to follow
this out,
having awakened at 4:00 this morning
because the air conditioning failed
as all transubstantiation
fails. I wonder
if for one minute I can leave my body
and enter a man dreaming
he loves his wife then wakes weeping
and strokes her hair *like the hand of solitude*
which feels the grief of others until its death,
but a man who also thinks
that if he rolls over on his left side
and dreams again
that it will be the reverse dream, that
he'll hate her as much as
he loved her before.

You need to know a few things:
that my friend's father was diagnosed as
having tuberculosis menengitis,
a rare virus of the brain,
that he's sole survivor
in the history of the disease, was given honorary
staff membership at Hershey Medical
Center, and twelve coupons for
a free spinal tap;
that his son, my friend, is 40 this August,
that he walks down seventeen rows
of corn at night just
to lose himself in the distance, just to know
the pain situated around the central
point of the nervous system,
at the point of junction between soul and body,
which goes on even through sleep,
never ceasing for a second.

*

I packed the stuff, loaded up, drove.
It seemed a falling backward
that falling
through meretricious pines and lawn ornaments.
The landscape took a beautiful shape or
was it pure sound or pure grief.
You suffer disembodied pain.
So you turn, you turn the ninety degrees of the Dipper,
bereft of self.
Is that the gravity Simone Weil
suffered for,
extinction of the self, weight which leadens in the legs,
which held her there looking up into the face
in the wish to see suffering exactly
as she suffered?

The source of man's moral energy is outside him, she wrote,
like that of food, air, etc.
He generally finds it, and that is why
he has the illusion. . . that his being
carries
the principle of its preservation.
So I wait in line at the hospital cafeteria
with my friend
and his father who once
played golf with Ike, and the old man
recounts
how once he stood *from one to eight in the morning*
for the sake of eating an egg: a base form
of virtue perhaps,
but the sky was perfect then,
something not to be forgotten. And I think of
how sound passes and disappears,
higher-pitched,
shorter wave-lengths at first
then longer and sadder.
Like an orchestra of trumpets standing
in an open car of a railroad train,
rushing
through the countryside, sailing
through the earth
in blackness.
I try to hear and see the lengthening
sound waves over the far,
white trees telling me to include hope
floating away. I watch the past
displace the future
long after the future has passed.
The train winds silently
uphill.
The trailing smoke's formation
whispers past itself.

*

The first nine months I do not exist I will
sing William, in your yellow
hair, where are you?
The old pines glisten.
I am weight on the passenger side
of the white Plymouth
droning
from the one good lake in Oklahoma.
Flaring and passing and gone,
I have come to kiss again
your sweet yellow head.
To bind
one thought with the other,
gravity with grace.

for Clint

Creeping Determinism

The way I marshall detail, no, fact,
believing I'm right long after
I'm wrong. Like replacing the windows
which don't need replacing. Measuring
with a tape from one edge to another
that new glass might let me see
what is there and not there.
But a pressure on the glass diverts
because of its metabolism. And
the eye caresses everything too openly.
The constant motion tires us, tires me—
the picture that my son had made, waking,
of a body so like my own but light, vibrant.
I cannot be cowardly or stupid, ever again.

Jarrell said the next time that they say
to me: he has your eyes I'll tell them
the truth: he has his own eyes. He
is the authority upon them
who notices a certain silence or lack
and calls out, "Mommy?" His eyes
find me bending, working
too intently on something which requires
his grace. Thinking incompletely, which
is to say, loving yet refusing to love, which is
the only way anyone *can* think. Now only the after-
image of the door closing, of my wife taking
our son to day care, of leaves swirling
like fingerprints of certitude and chance.

The Man in the Boy's Storm

> Such is the nature of force. Its power
> to transform a man into a thing is double
> and cuts both ways; it petrifies differently,
> but equally, the souls of those who suffer
> it and of those who wield it.
> —*Simone Weil, "The Iliad:
> Poem of Force"*

I'm opening the cellar door which doesn't
fly off its hinges to see the tornado,
the afternoon light, green with wanting
to be something else, grass under sun
maybe but green and pink and shiny,
its funnel too far away, the air
so still I hear the future tick
like that watch I drop decades later
in freezing mud out back while lifting or
fixing something like changing the plugs
or changing the oil in the Datsun. My family
sits in dark with other families, piously
it seems, but with minds open with wide terror
that we are here for grace of charity of our neighbors—
we don't own the cellar, nor our
fidgeting childhood, nor the air we imagine
as elastic as a Tribune rubberband. Later than
I can even imagine I watch my son complain
that his fingers are tangled, inventing
jailer and lock. When I tell him about
air which hung like famous, futuristic berries
he knows I'm lying. When I tell him
about my own father who snored from under
the bed, I think, when the tornado came,
knowing a little peace, some information will pass
and make a swinging kind of motion, as if its
bough were about to break, and sky
unhinge. Someone would say, Close
that door, kid. And it wouldn't be as if

it weren't raining, though it had been
a little. It would be as if he were just
beginning to hear some automatic, chthonic
roar. Like a train, they say, like some
woman from somewhere in the dark might say
something he couldn't hear at first. He's
in the present tense listening to something
which gradually makes itself known and felt
like the noise of power, where no one can live
or even dream completely. And the sun is up.
And the noise she sings is powerful, is song.

NOTES

"The Shimmer of Influence" refers to Ben Jonson's "On My First Son" and borrows a phrase in the last line from a poem by Dave Smith.

In "The Persistence of Influence," certain lines refer to *The Odyssey.*

"The Anxiety of Influence" takes its title from the critical book by Harold Bloom.

The phrase "Mozart's Starling" refers to the composer's pet, whose song was reputed to have inspired the 17th Symphony. Mozart claimed that the symphony was an exact duplication of the starling's song.

In "Lullaby," certain lines of the poem are inspired by Melville's "After the Pleasure Party" and by Robert Penn Warren's "Promises."

The Strings, or string theory, is a sub-atomic theory which some physicists believe might explain the beginning of the universe and, by implication, its end.

In "For Luck," Sheridan Avenue is a through street in Tulsa, Oklahoma.

In "Luck," certain parts of the poem owe to Pascal's "The Mind of a Geometrician," Yeats's "Song of Wandering Angus" and "The Fisherman," Boethius's *Consolation of Philosophy,* Eliot's *Four Quartets,* Pound's later discussion of *The Cantos,* Whitman's "Starting from Paumanok" and "Song of Myself," Santayana, and Mallarmé.

In "The Distance," certain lines refer to Simone Weil's post-humously published *Gravity and Grace;* and the quotation, "La mia solitudine l'atrui dolore germivo fino all morte. . . ." appears on a small plaque attached to Weil's gravestone by an anonymous donor.

"Creeping Determinism"—When cause takes on a salience.

Ralph Burns's first book, *Us,* won the Great Lakes Colleges Award (1983). His second book, *Any Given Day,* was published by The University of Alabama Press in 1985. His poems have appeared in *Poetry, The Atlantic, The Ohio Review, Field,* and many other magazines. He currently teaches at the University of Arkansas at Little Rock.